A Life of Triumph

by
Esther Weber

 Mazo Publishers
Jerusalem, Israel

A Life Of Triumph

Text Copyright © 2007 Esther Weber

ISBN: 978-965-7344-16-3 - Soft Cover
ISBN: 978-965-7344-23-1 - Hard Cover

Published by:
Mazo Publishers
Chaim Mazo, Publisher
P.O. Box 36084
Jerusalem 91360 Israel

Website: www.mazopublishers.com
Email: info@mazopublishers.com
USA: 1-815-301-3559
Israel: 054-7294-565

Contact the Author
Esther Weber
Email: irwinweber200@aol.com

Printed In Israel

To my Husband Irwin,
my Children, and Grandchildren

Contents

Acknowledgments

First and foremost, *to my loving husband, Irwin,* without your help and support, I would never have developed into the woman that I am today.

To my children: David, Michelle, and Debbie who are, and always have been my life, and purpose of my entire existence. And to their spouses: Aviva, Michael, and Yossi, my love and gratitude for the added joy that they have brought to our family.

To my adoring and adorable grandchildren: Daniella, Avi, Amir, Rachel, Adam, Haley, Benjamin, Aiden, Arielle, and Skye who have my unconditional love now and forever.

To Shoshana Marks, without whom this book would never have been written.

To Minda Fisher, who has come into my life at this late stage and who has shown me the meaning of a true and loving friendship.

To my sister-in-law, Selly, who has always been there for me and my entire family.

To my dear Aunt Eva, without whose clarity of mind, courage, and dedication, I would never have survived.

I love you all!

Esther

Foreword

For 50 years, the world kept quiet about the genocide of millions of Jews in the Holocaust in Europe during World War II. There was complete silence about what happened in the Concentration Camps and absolutely nothing was taught in the schools until the late 1980s.

For me, having spent most of my childhood years in hiding, the trauma of my experience has been like a bomb inside of me waiting to explode. By the time I was liberated, I could not speak about it – not a word. This was an experience which I might, on occasion, share with other survivors, but not with the "outside world." It was too painful for me to say anything about it, to expose any part of it.

I also feared that speaking about it would set me apart from my friends and surroundings. It would arouse in me the intense discomfort of having people feel sorry for me, would make me relive my experiences over and over again. This would consume me, would force me to look back, would block out my prospects of a normal future, would disturb the lives of my children, and would forever prevent me from extricating myself from my past. It would also expose my vulnerability to public view, thus revealing, not only my physical nakedness, but more painfully, the wounds engraved on my soul as a Jew and a human being.

I kept silent for 39 years. Even friends were unaware that I was a survivor. The first time I spoke of the Holocaust was when I was approached to give a deposition to the Steven Spielberg project. Only then was I able to summon the strength to speak about it.

At this time, because I am among the last of the living survivors, I feel that it is my duty to tell my story to you, my children and grandchildren, and to the young generation of today so that something like this will never happen again.

Esther

Quotes And Letters

Dear Esther,

As the son of Holocaust survivors, I am just amazed at the sheer force of will and determination you displayed at such a young age and continue to demonstrate every day. I have seen so many survivors lost in nightmares of depression and anger, and here you are, powerfully living the words of the famous command of all IDF officers, "Follow me!"

Follow me as I build a new life on my own.

Follow me as I partner up with a spouse who shares my enthusiasm for all the good life has to offer.

Follow me as I rise out of the ashes of the Shoah and raise a beautiful family.

Follow me as I help Israel in all her times of need.

Follow me as I explore new experiences with the excitement of a child undiminished and unblemished by time and experience.

S. Rubinfeld

Dear Esther,

You have wisdom, you have bitachon, and you have inspiration. You have so much to offer Klal Yisrael with your experiences. You have touched my heart. All you need is a pen and paper to tell your story.

Shoshana Mark

Dear Esther,

"You are an inspiration. The days of your youth were less than ideal, yet you have been able to rise above the challenges of your young days and focus on the good qualities in people, and not dwell on the anger that many would have.

"*A Life Of Triumph* is an amazing story. It has changed my son's life. He is absolutely astonished that you went through such a journey as a young child, and today hold no ill feelings towards those who caused you the discomfort. He has stated that before speaking with you, he did not really understand the meaning of forgiveness, but now realizes that he can overcome any obstacles in life. He said, 'if Mrs. Weber has been able to overcome what she went through, anything that will challenge me, will be easy.'"

T. Strauss

Dear Esther,

I just finished reading your memoir for the third time, and I can't tell you how moving it is! You have done a marvellous job of telling your life story – your wonderful relationship with your husband Irwin, and how you're interested in everything and everyone!

I'm so proud of you – it takes a lot of courage to go back in time and review all the hardships that you went through.

Love,
Marion Talansky

FRIENDS OF ISRAEL DISABLED WAR VETERANS

(Beit Halochem)
15 E. 26 St. • Suite 904 • New York, N.Y. 10010
(212) 689-3220 • Fax (212) 689-3236

April 7, 1995

Mr. & Mrs. Irwin Weber
7 Boxwood Lane
Lawrence, New York 11559

Dear Esther & Irwin:

When the Lebanese War caused catastrophic numbers of
Israeli casualties, you, Esther, flew to Israel and
served as a hospital volunteer, ministering daily to
the needs of an entire ward of wounded soldiers.

And you felt such compassion, affection and respect for
those men that you invited them all to the States. You
and Irwin hosted their memorable trip and you created
friends for a lifetime.

They will never forget you.

When the cause of Israel's disabled war veterans, who
now number 40,000, was invisible in the USA, you were
among the advanced guard who trumpeted their
rehabilitation needs to all your friends. And you
continue to serve as their advocates to this very day.

For all these accomplishments, we will not forget you.

I am very pleased that Congregation Kneseth Israel
recognizes your unique contributions to our cause, to
the State of Israel, and to your community.

Mazal Tov on this honor you so well deserve.

Sincerely,

Sy Colen
Executive Vice President

SC/bwk

Friends Supports Beit Halochem Sports, Rehabilitation & Social Centers
In Tel Aviv, Haifa & Jerusalem; & The Beit Kay Rest Home In Nahariya.

SURVIVORS OF THE
SⁿHאOˡAשH
VISUAL HISTORY FOUNDATION℠

16 July 1998

Esther Weber
7 Boxwood Lane
Lawrence, NY 11559

Dear Mrs. Weber,

Thank you for contributing your testimony to Survivors of the Shoah Visual History Foundation. In sharing your story, you have granted future generations the opportunity to experience a direct connection with history.

Your interview will be carefully preserved as an important part of the most comprehensive library of Holocaust testimonies ever assembled. Far into the future, people will be able to see a face, hear a voice, and observe a life, so that they may listen and learn, and always remember.

Thank you for your invaluable contribution, your strength, and your generosity of spirit.

All my best,

Steven Spielberg
Chairman

Jerusalem, 29 November 2005

Ms. Esther Weber
7 Boxwood Lane
Lawrence N.Y. 11559
USA

Dear Ms. Weber,

Thank you very much for sending me your life story. The account of your survival and triumph testifies to the need to remember the past as part of our shaping the future. Your family's story which spans over three continents, as well as your strong love and connection to the State of Israel are most impressive and I congratulate you on this publication. It is this very spirit that guides us in our work at Yad Vashem – to transmit the message of Holocaust remembrance and to fill it with content and depth in order to inspire the younger generations.

I will forward your publication to our library, where it will be made available to the many researchers, educators, students and others who use our facilities. Yad Vashem's library not only seeks to serve its readers today, but it is a repository for published and book–form information about the Holocaust and related events for the generations to come.

Best wishes,

Avner Shalev
Chairman, Yad Vashem Directorate

A Life of Triumph

Chapter One

Born Into A War

I was born on September 28, 1937, in a small town (a dorf) called Vengluvka. My parents were married in 1935, two years short of my birth. My mother Dvorah Silberman came from a family of eight children – five girls and three boys. Her mother, my Grandmother Esther, died at a young age. My Grandfather Itzhak, a handsome strong man, was left to take care of his eight children alone. His two sons, Toivie and Sam, were sent to America to seek a better life, followed by their sister Mollie who arrived some years later. Another daughter Rivkah went off to Palestine and the rest of the family remained in Poland. My mother Dvorah was the youngest of all her siblings – she was still single.

My father's hometown was Krzemienica, also a small town near Mielitz. As the story was told to me, he was accused of stealing a horse. With the threat of death if he was caught, he ran away from home and found his way to Vengluvka, a small shtetl where he was taken in and hidden at a cousin's house. In time when things quieted down, his uncle introduced him to a neighbor's daughter – my mother, Dvorah Silberman.

My mother's older sister Miriam was already married and living in a nearby city, Krosno. She was four years older than my mother and she took on the task of

Grandfather Itzhak Silverman (center, third from left) with family

arranging the wedding for my parents in her home. It was a great *simcha* (celebration) and all the family came from different parts of the country. Some came on horse-back. One cousin, Murray Hollander came by bicycle (50 kilometers) from a town called Tarnoff.

My parents then settled in my Grandfather's home in Vengluvka where, two years later in 1937, I was born. It was a joyful and happy existence for a young couple with a new baby. Who could possibly predict that a terrible catastrophe was already looming on the horizon? Who could imagine that Europe and the world would soon be caught up in a world war with Germany?

Shortly after my birth, anti-Semitism began to show its ugly face. The Germans invaded Poland in 1939 and the Jews became the scapegoats as in every previous generation.

With discrimination, loss of jobs, persecution and threat of death all around them, my Aunt Miriam and her daughter Ciporah went into hiding, while Ciporah's father joined the Polish Army. He was later wounded somewhere on the Russian Front, where he eventually succumbed and died of his injuries.

Wedding picture of my mother and father in 1936

My Aunt Miriam wanted my mother to join her and Ciporah in the cellar where they were hiding, but my mother, the free spirit that she was, refused to live underground like a rat. She chose instead to try her luck at a working camp in Germany. On her way there, she and many others like her, were taken off the train in a town called Dembica by the S.S. The German Secret Service questioned her and demanded to see her Polish Identification Papers – which of course she didn't have since she was a Jew. At that point the German took out his revolver, pulled the trigger and snuffed out an innocent Jewish life.

My mother in 1936

My mother was murdered at the young age of 27. There are days I wish I could see my mother's face again. I can only recall her holding me and singing a children's lullaby – "*Ai lulli lulli, shloff mein kindalle shloff* – Sleep my baby, sleep." Try as I might, I can't picture my mother now but I feel it was my mother who sang that song to me and for a short period of our lives together gave me the love and nurturing that sustained me all my life.

Another one of my earliest memories are of my father taking me to my grandparents house (his parents, Moshe and Ita Muhlbauer). One Friday evening (erev Shabbat), the Shabbat candles were lit and the glow of the candles gave off a warm and cozy feeling. Everyone was happy and at peace. Suddenly the Gestapo (S.S.) soldiers barged in, grabbed my aging grandfather by the beard. They cursed the dirty Jew, lit a match to his beard, and set him on fire. I can still hear those painful horrifying screams fill the entire household. I was no more than a year and a half but I've never forgotten this horror.

At this time my father decided that the only way to save his child was to bring me to the home of his schoolboy friend, Joseph Bik and his family. My father's only hope was that the Polish family would possibly take in and save a Jewish child – his child. My parents' decision to each go their separate ways in order to save their only child was a noble but doubtless very painful decision. My mother never lived to see the results of that decision. The following is what my father told me years later.

My father wrapped the baby (me) in blankets, and started out on his long and dangerous journey from Vengluvka to Krzemienica by horse and wagon and then continued by train. At one point of this journey, he sat in the train station with me in his arms waiting for the train to arrive. Suddenly an S.S. officer appeared. My father who had no Polish documents was sure that this was the end for both of us. The officer approached him and asked him where he was going. My father told him he was taking his sick baby to a hospital in Mielitz. Before the officer had a chance to ask any more questions, my father offered to buy him a drink at a bar. This was a clever decision for while they were having their drink, a young lady sat down next to them. My father bought her a drink too and she and the Gestapo struck up a conversation that went something like this. "We're looking for these dirty Jews who are hiding in every corner like rats. They never suspected my father of being one of these "rats." While the German was busy with his new friend, the train arrived, my father bid them good-bye and for that day, our lives were spared. To this day, I don't know if it was my father's clever quick thinking or just plain sheer luck that saved us both but for sure it was G-d's will that we survived another day.

When we arrived at the home of the Bik Family, my father explained the situation to his friend Joseph and the family. He told them that without their help there was no way either of us would survive.

The year was 1940 and I was just about three years old. Reluctantly, the Bik Family agreed to take me in and to raise me as their own. This of course meant that I would be reared Christian – taken to church, taught all the prayers, Baptized, etc. etc. My father agreed to everything just to keep me alive. But, his parting words to me were "Always remember that you are Jewish but don't ever reveal this secret to anyone because they will kill you – promise?" I promised. I heard my father's words and although I was only three years old, I kept this secret and promise all the days of my life.

My father came to visit me only one more time and then I never saw him again. He couldn't come to visit me anymore because he was afraid that they would give me back to him and what would he do then? After leaving me with the Bik Family, my father found out that his parents and his sisters Chavah (Eva) and Gittel were deported to a nearby town called Bieshatka and rounded

The Bik Family farm

up into a Ghetto. Eva escaped miraculously but his sister Gittel and his parents were sent to a concentration camp where they all perished. My father's other brother Meyer who lived in Mielitz with his wife and children, were caught by the Nazis. They were tortured and killed as well.

My father and his younger brother Shiah, went back to their home. Their Polish neighbors warned them to leave immediately, but they decided to spend the night there and leave the next day. Unfortunately, while they were asleep, the Gestapo barged in, started shouting – Shiah, who was a young, handsome boy of 17, was killed immediately. My father jumped out of the window, miraculously escaped a spray of bullets and ran and ran into the deep forest where he hid out till nightfall. This was a way of life and death for all Jews. They were hunted like dogs and when found, killed on the spot without the slightest provocation – their only crime was that they were born "Jews."

My daughter, Michelle Susan, was named for my father's young brother Shiah, whose life ended before he had a chance to live it. But our daughter, Malka Sheine, is a beautiful symbol of a beautiful soul that will always be kept alive and remembered through her and through her children – Aidan, Arielle, and Shachar (Skye).

My life with the Bik family proceeded normally. I went to church every Sunday. I even sang in a choir. I kneeled every night and said my prayers diligently. I knew I had to be a good girl because I was taught that there was a Heaven and Hell and I knew that I would have to confess all my sins to the Priest when I got older. I was very religious. Nevertheless, I knew I was Jewish but remembering my father's parting words, I never revealed my true identity to anyone.

At this time, living with the Bik Family on their farm, my job was to oversee the cows grazing in the open fields. My true test came one day when while tending to the cattle, I was spotted by some Polish teenagers who called me by my Polish name Aniushka. When I realized that they saw me I immediately jumped into a nearby ditch and tried to hide. I stayed there till they left and then went home. Unfortunately the damage was already done. The boys went to the police and reported the Bik Family for hiding a Jewish child. The police notified them that they had 24 hours to get rid of me or they would burn down the farm and kill everyone in it.

That night I was hidden in the animal shed and there was sadness throughout the house. I remember the family including the male members all crying. Apparently, they had grown attached to me and I to them as well. The parting would be very difficult for all of us.

In the morning, we boarded a train to Warsaw to find my father's sister (my Aunt Eva). She was a young girl herself, 18 years old living with a Polish family. Hiding the fact that she was Jewish, she supported herself by working as a seamstress for another Polish family. She had false Polish Papers and luckily, she looked Polish as did I. The Bik Family explained the situation to her – that I was recognized and they couldn't keep me any longer and they had no one else to turn to. My father was nowhere to be found. My aunt was very reluctant to take me as she was desperately trying to save her own life but there was no one else and so she had no choice. I was after all, her brother's child.

And so, this began our new struggle for survival in Warsaw. My Aunt Eva became my new guardian and my mother. According to some of her stories today, I was not easy to take care of.

I was very much a tomboy and one day I beat up a boy who was twice my size. The mother came to complain to my aunt and my aunt gave me a good spanking. I was always playing with boys because they did things that were more fun than girls – running, jumping, climbing trees, etc. One day I fell out of a tree and ripped open my whole knee. I still have the scars to prove it. I would walk around whistling like a boy and I remember being reprimanded for not behaving like a girl.

After one of my serious scoldings by my poor exasperated aunt, my teary retort to her was "if my mother was here, she wouldn't treat me like this." My poor Aunt Eva was devastated and guilt-ridden. She never laid a hand on me again. She hugged me instead and we both cried ourselves to sleep.

The year was now 1942 and we were being bombed by the Allies day and night. I will never forget the screaming sound of the low flying planes followed by a loud "Boom" of the bombs. The sound of the planes was just as terrifying as the actual explosion of the bombs that followed.

My Aunt Eva and I were living with a Polish family in Warsaw – the capital of Poland. The husband knew my aunt from before the war. He was also instrumental in helping to get her false documents stating that she was Christian.

His wife, however, was never aware of us being Jewish. My aunt had an outside job working for another family and I was left alone under the care of this Polish woman who resented having to take care of a child even though she was well paid for her services. To say that I was being abused by this woman is an understatement. I was five years old now and my greatest fear was being deserted by my aunt. My fear each day was that she would go to work and not come back for me.

We lived close to the Warsaw Ghetto. The sight of babies wrapped in blankets being thrown from the windows and mothers screams followed by gunshots were ever present. It was as if the Nazis used these poor babies for shooting practice. Unfortunately, their aim was very accurate. Within minutes, the mothers followed their babies to their death.

Walking in the street and stepping over dead bodies covered by flies were sights that will remain with me all my life. When I was five years old, I couldn't understand how those people lying there in the street covered by flies buzzing all around them didn't move and try to shake the flies off their bodies. Didn't it itch them? Not until many years later did I realize how the sight of these dead bodies affected me.

[About thirty-five years later – married and living in New York – I saw a tragic event take place before my eyes. A man, a total stranger passed out and died before my eyes and I went into shock – not realizing then the effects of my childhood on my psyche (sub-conscious). Evidently, the sight of this stranger lying dead on the ground, brought back memories that were long buried in my subconscious. For years, I tried to bury my past and lived as though I was not affected by it, but eventually the past caught up with me. But now back to Warsaw and the war.]

Another time, during a bombing raid we all had to go into our bunkers – my aunt was at work and I was with this Polish woman who would beat and abuse me at the slightest provocation. This time I had to go to the bathroom but there was none in the underground bunker. Rather than soiling myself and getting beaten for it, I ran upstairs into the building, not thinking I could be killed by the bombs that were coming down and exploding all around me.

One day when I couldn't take the daily beatings anymore, I ran away from home. My aunt had a lady friend who lived near us but the problem was that there was a deep black forest between our home and where she lived. I ventured deep into the forest and got lost there. I tried to get out but each turn led me deeper and deeper into the forest. When I couldn't find my way out, I sat down on a tree stump and accepted my fate. I was familiar with the tale of the "Little Red Riding Hood" and so I was sure a wolf would come along and eat me up. There was another popular Polish tale about gypsies who kidnapped children, dipped them in brown water and they were never returned to their respective homes. My thoughts about never being found by my aunt ran rampant – and my child's fear took over my whole being. All I could do was to sit there and cry. When I realized I had no other choice but to try again, I started walking in one direction, till I saw some light between the trees – I followed the light and eventually found my way out of the deep dark forest and returned home.

During one hot summer, my head and my whole body was covered with lice. The Polish woman never bothered to clean me. Instead she took a razor and shaved my head so when my aunt came home from work she saw my beautiful curls were gone and I was left with a bald head. The children in the street laughed and

made fun of me. I didn't want to leave the house. Eventually my aunt gave me a hat to wear till my hair grew back. Though it was a very hot and uncomfortable summer I wouldn't leave the house without wearing the hat.

In spite of all these events, I was under the impression that I had a normal childhood. At the end of 1944 and start of 1945, the war was coming to an end.

The Germans were on the run, being chased by the Russian army. Because the Germans didn't want any witnesses to their atrocities, they began rounding up the citizens of Warsaw, us amongst them. We were taken out of the city and lead in a death march towards the gas chambers. My aunt and I were on this line from which there was no escape. If you tried to run, you were shot on the spot. If you couldn't keep up with the rest, you were shot and I saw many people killed for no reason but they were too weak, too sick, or too old to continue. Seeing people killed became an ordinary event.

At the age of seven, death, torture and pain became part of my normal psyche.

Suddenly the line stopped at a nearby farmhouse. My aunt in her usual wisdom bribed one of the guards to let us remain in back of the line. This decision, as it turned out, saved our lives once more. When the line started to move, we ran

Ciporah and I with our friend Ruthie

and hid in a nearby ditch till nightfall when it was safe to come out. By some miracle we were spared once again.

The war ended in May 1945. I was seven and a half, going on eight. Our liberation came at the hands of the Russian Army. As with all refugees, my aunt and I began our long trek back to our hometown of Krzemienica – my aunt brought me back to the place where my father had left me at the start of the war.

When we arrived at the Bik family farm, my first reaction was to go to the church, get down on my hands and knees and pray. Suddenly, I looked up and saw my father standing over me. We had both survived this terrible holocaust – once again we found each other. Once again, we were a family. My mother (*zt'l*), was gone and my father became once more the center of my world.

As with most holocaust survivors, my father decided to leave our birthplace Poland forever. But the process of leaving Poland was a hard and very difficult journey mostly by foot over mountains and valleys – in the bitter cold of a European winter. I remember being hungry and cold all the time, but my father's kindness and patience was what I remember

Ciporah and I with a doll

ber mostly. I loved my father with all my heart and wanted to keep him near me forever. I never dreamed we would separate ever again.

After we left the Bik family and Krzemienica, we continued to Krosno, which was my mother's birthplace. There we found her sister Miriam and her daughter Ciporah. We arrived at the time of the Jewish holiday of Pesach. Survivors came back to their original homes and that's the way they found out who was left alive and who was gone. My father took me with him to a makeshift synagogue and at the age of eight I began saying Yiskor for my mother, the prayer for the dead. I was the only child there. I did not know what the prayer meant but my father told me I would be saying it for the rest of my life during certain Jewish Holidays. On several occasions, I tried to convince my father to move to another city and convert to Christianity. I continued wearing my cross, hoping my father would agree to my plan. I just wanted to live and I was constantly living with the fear of being killed.

The war was over, but the Pogroms continued. Jews were still being persecuted and killed, even though the war was over and Hitler was defeated as was Germany.

I performed on stage, doing the "Kozatzka."

One evening we were celebrating a wedding when suddenly a bunch of hooligans burst into the room and began lining us all up against the wall, threatening to shoot us all. Somehow my father climbed up to the roof of the building and shouted for the police – who arrived just in time to rescue us. This was just another life-saving miracle.

Time passed and we left Poland via Czechoslovakia, Hungary and Austria. My Aunt Miriam, my cousin Ciporah, my father, and I finally arrived in Saltzburgh, Austria where we found our cousins, Murray and Rose Hollander. They welcomed us warmly and we stayed with them a few months. From there my aunt and my cousin left for Italy, then to Cypress and eventually to Israel, while my father and I took another direction to Germany. Our eventual destination was to the United States of America.

In Germany, we met up with my Aunt Eva (my father's sister) who by this time had gotten married to a

Wedding picture of Aunt Eva and Uncle Julius Merkrebs

young man, Julius Merkrebs. They lived in a DP Camp (Displaced Persons) in Landsberg. The year was 1946. We moved in with them temporarily, while we waited for our American Visas to come through. This was a very happy time for me because I was with my father and once again reunited with my Aunt Eva, whom I adored. I thought my happiness would last forever, but it was not to be.

My father learned of a program that was set up by an organization called the HIASS that sent orphans out of Europe first. So he registered me with this organization with the intention to follow me to America soon after.

Inside the DP Camp in Landsberg

This photo was taken by an American journalist and published in the New York Times, 1946

On the way to ballet class with my friend

Chapter Two

Journey To Freedom

I lived temporarily in a town called Prien Am Lech while awaiting my turn to leave Germany. I was the youngest or-phan there. It was March 1948. I was ten and a half years old. The time for me to leave Germany and the only family I knew had arrived. My father and my Aunt Eva escorted me to a port in town

Identity Card – February 26, 1948
Notice Nationality – Jew

Orphanage in Prien, Germany. I'm in the center

called Bremen Haven. I was to meet the ship that would take me to my new destination – my new world – America. I said good-bye to my only family and boarded the ship with a group of total strangers. I wasn't sad because I knew my father would be following me soon after. I was told that a family would await me in America and I would live with them till my father arrived. I had no reason to believe otherwise. However, destiny took a different turn.

As the ship sailed away from the harbor, I saw myself separating from the only world I knew and sadness overtook me – the further we moved away from the harbor, the more I began to feel alone. My father never saw my tears and I never knew his heartbreak. My father felt he was sending me to a better life in America. He did what he felt was best for me. Who's to say what's right and what's wrong with decisions we make in life?

*Father and I
just before I left Germany*

My feelings were never considered in these decisions. As always, I did what I was told to do.

I must describe my three-week journey from Bremen Haven, Germany to Ellis Island, U.S.A. on the open seas. The name of our boat was "The Marine Marlin." Needless to say it wasn't a luxury liner. I believe I was the youngest child on the boat. At least I didn't see anyone else my age. After a few days at sea, I didn't see anyone at all, since most everyone was seasick because of the constant storms and bad weather.

One day I came out on the deck to get some fresh air but the seas were very rough and the deck of the ship was very slippery. I nearly slipped off the deck and fell overboard. I grabbed a rail and hung on for dear life. Had I fallen overboard, no one would have known the difference and I wouldn't have been missed by anyone. G-d was watching over me once more.

In my childish way of thinking, I was quite proud of myself that I was the only one that didn't get seasick

– but eventually my turn came as well. The nausea and vomiting was not pleasant, but there was no one to complain to so I took care of myself as best as I could and I survived.

I had heard stories about whales (great big ones), turning over entire ships at sea, so a feeling of fear suddenly came over me. I didn't go out on the deck again after that.

One night there was a general alarm and everyone was told to appear on deck. We had to don our life jackets – it was pitch black outside and the sirens were ringing to warn us of the impending danger. We were heading straight for an iceberg. Luckily the captain was able to maneuver the ship and avoided a real catastrophe. The month of March was very dangerous for the winter was over and the icebergs were very common since the ice that was frozen was beginning to melt and float freely.

We were nearing the Canadian Coast, Halifax to be exact, when we heard a great commotion on board. It seems that there were two stowaways on board. They were brought before a team of medical doctors and upon examination found to have Syphilis, a sexual disease – I didn't know what sex was so it made no difference to me. They were taken off the boat in Halifax and sent back to Germany on the next boat.

After that incident, we were all afraid that by the time we arrived in the U.S., we too could be sent back to Europe at the slightest sign of illness. The American health codes for immigrants were very strict.

Upon waking up on the morning of April 10, 1948, we were all very excited because we knew we were nearing the New York Harbor. As we came closer, we caught the first glimpse of the Statue of Liberty and the lights of New York Harbor. It was the most beautiful sight I had ever seen. I knew then that this would be my home for the rest of my life. This was the last stop of a long and difficult journey. I was ten and a half years old and about to begin a new life, not anticipating how difficult that new life would be.

The Statue of Liberty

Chapter Three

Growing Up In America

At Ellis Island we were processed and examined by several different doctors and there transported to different parts of the country. I was taken to an orphanage somewhere in the Bronx to wait for a family member to come and claim me.

After two weeks in the orphanage, I was met by my father's uncle, Victor Seiden who took me to his home in Williamsburgh, Brooklyn, where I met my first American family. I didn't speak a word of English, only Polish, Yiddish and German. So we conversed in Yiddish. Their two children Evelyn and Nathan and their mother Sarah, were very welcoming. They enrolled me in public school in the fifth grade according to my age. I can't imagine how I actually managed without the language, but in time English grammar and spelling became my best subjects.

I was eager to be accepted as an American – I didn't want to be pitied because I was a refugee. I worked very hard at losing my accent.

Just as I was getting adjusted to school and my new life, I received the shock of my life. A letter arrived from my father telling me that the moment I had waited for from the minute I said good-bye to him in Germany was not to be. He would be changing course and not

Cousin Evelyn Seiden
and I, 1948

Cousin Nathan Seiden
with Aunt Sarah

Uncle Victor Seiden, Irene Merkrebs on my lap,
Aunt Eva & Uncle Julius, 1951

A New Year card from my father, 1948

coming to America after all, but rather he would be going on to Israel to marry my Aunt Miriam. Needless to say, I was devastated.

Now I knew I was totally alone in the world. I was eleven years old. Being abandoned by your only surviving parent at such an impressionable age is not something that's easy to accept. But accept it I did, as always, and I went on. I knew I had to carve out a life for myself and after days and weeks of crying myself to sleep, I made up my mind that I wouldn't give up. I would go on living and would prove to everyone that I would amount to something someday and that a day would come when everyone would be proud of me – and I would survive.

I did well in school. I decided that I had to be a very good girl and to behave well so that my family would have no problems with me. I did everything that was expected of me. When at times, I did misbehave, I was told that if I didn't like my situation, I could go to my father in Israel, which I knew was not possible. I was always told and reminded how lucky I was to be in

America – I felt very much alone but I kept it to myself.

After two years with the Seiden Family, I was moved to another family on the Lower East Side – 255 Rivington Street. This was another aunt and uncle – my mother's brother Toivie Silverman and his wife Fannie. One day when I was about fourteen, I sat with my Aunt Fannie – she was very kind and I felt I could pour out to her about some of my wartime experiences. As she was an American-born woman, she was very limited in her understanding of Europe and what went on during the war there.

I proceeded to tell her how we had nothing to eat for five years other than some dried bread and water, some goat milk and whatever could be scraped together in the streets. Sometimes we'd find a dead animal, such as a horse or a cow and that served as a meal for days – maybe weeks. If you weren't killed by a bullet, you died

Father, Ciporah, and Aunt Miriam

*Graduation from
Junior High PS 188*

of starvation. For anyone to have survived this horror was a miracle. After listening to some of my experiences, her reply was simply "what do you think, we here in America had it so good? We too suffered because of the war. We had to wait on line for coffee, sugar, etc., etc."

At this point, I realized that there was no use speaking to anyone about what we went through. These Americans couldn't possibly understand our plight. I never spoke about the subject of the Holocaust again.

Two years passed and I started Seward Park High School. Halfway through, I had to move again. This time to live with another aunt and uncle in the Bronx. Mollie and Max Greenspan – my mother's sister. They

*Aunt Eva, Aunt Fannie
Silverman & I, 1952*

*Cousins Phil and Esther, Uncle Max, Cousin Harold,
and Aunt Mollie Greenspan, 1953*

took me in because their son Harold was serving in the
Korean War and they had a spare room for me.

But, when he came home from Korea, they decided
that it wasn't "healthy" for a young sixteen-year-old to

Friend Sandy and I, 1954 – My teenage years

be living under the same roof with her cousin who was in his twenties. I couldn't understand this thinking since my cousin Harold saw me as his little kid sister and I looked upon him as my big brother.

I was still in high school and working after school to support myself when I decided to move out of my aunt's house, since I wasn't welcome there anymore. I moved into a rooming house with my friend's grandparents. This was the end of my shuttling from house to house. From the day I arrived in America, I knew I wasn't wanted by anyone. My father and Aunt Miriam never sent for me and I had nowhere else to go. Now I was finishing high school and could become self-sufficient.

At this point, I had been dating my boyfriend Irwin Weber and though we were both very young – I was seventeen and he was eighteen, we decided to get married. Our wedding took place on December 22, 1956. They say marriages at such a young age don't last. Well, they're wrong. You must know yourself well, and choose a partner for life that has the values and the character that you admire in a person. Add to that equation love and friendship and mutual respect, the answer has to be a beautiful lifelong relationship.

After forty-eight years of marriage, three wonderful children, David, Michelle, and Debbie and their wonderful spouses, Aviva Stavish, Yossi Hadad and Michael Schreiber, plus ten beautiful grandchildren, Daniella, Avi, Josh, Rachel, Adam, Haley, Benjamin, Aiden, Arielle and the latest addition, little "Skye," I can today attest to a successful marriage till 120.

Chapter Four

The Start Of A New Way Of Life

Now I will begin the story of the second and new part of my life. It is a partnership with my husband Irwin that I know will never end.

Before I start, I must add a few words about my courtship with Irwin. First of all, I never went out with any guys who were Holocaust survivors. Why? Because as I said before, I set out on a path to leave my past behind me. I wanted to be an All-American-Girl – Rock & Roll, etc. When I met Irwin, he never knew I was a Holocaust survivor. I had no accent and the subject never came up. I was not proud of my refugee status and didn't like being called the "greener couziner," not even in jest.

Irwin and I

Today things are different. Times have changed drastically – for the better, I might add. But in 1948, when I arrived in America, I was a refugee, a new immigrant in the New World. This was a stigma I was determined to overcome.

By the time I graduated Seward Park High School, I was already dating Irwin seriously. Though we were both very young and in love, I seventeen, he eighteen, we spoke of a future together.

Irwin was everything I ever dreamed of in a mate. He was handsome, kind, generous, supportive and above all, a "sport" – I knew I could always depend on him and that he would

always be there for me. Other than losing his hair, nothing about him has changed through the years.

Irwin brought me home to meet his parents and my future in-laws, Abe and Ruthie Weber as well as his sister Selma.

After meeting his family, Irwin insisted I meet with his "Extended Family." These were people whom he felt very close to through the years – Blanche and Jack Mittleman – and their sister  and brother-in-law Sylvia and Phil Hiatt. These two couples not only were Irwin's friends, but his "mentors" as well, and he adored them then as he adores them now.

Phil Hiatt was, and still is a Rabbi as well as a wonderful teacher. More importantly, Phil was the most influential person at this point in my life. He sat me down and discussed with me the beauty and importance of a religious Jewish life. He explained everything to me in such a nice and welcoming way that I immediately felt comfortable in this new environment. "Phil, you made a nice Jewish girl out of me and I'm not sorry. Irwin and I are grateful to you till today."

Irwin and I were married December 22, 1956

We were married two years later. My wedding was a mixture of happiness and sadness. I knew that my father would not be the one to walk me down the aisle

since he couldn't leave Israel. Standing there all alone, it suddenly hit me.

Though my Aunt Eva and her husband Uncle Julius escorted me down the aisle, it wasn't a substitute for a child being led down the aisle by her parents. While under the Chupah, it was the first time I felt I was truly an orphan. I was only nineteen, and my emotions were playing havoc with the reality of my life. The tears were rolling down my cheeks. I was not only facing my new future with my new husband, but a new way of life as well.

Irwin was brought up Orthodox and there was no question which direction our life together would take. Though I knew who I was and what it meant to be Jewish, an Orthodox life never occurred to me. But I wasn't about to change this man who meant the world to me. The Feminist Movement didn't exist for me so whatever way of life my husband followed, that would be my way of life as well.

Though I had no formal Hebrew education, I poured over the "Shulchan Aruch" and a few other books of Jewish Law and I acquired the education that a Jewish woman needs to keep a Jewish Orthodox home – Kashruth, Shabbat, etc. etc. My Jewishness was self-taught tempered with my basic common sense. I was transformed into an Orthodox Jewish housefrau.

I went on with my life and at age twenty-one, I had my first child, David. Motherhood hit me very hard. It was now that I really began thinking about my mother *(zt'l),* who never lived to see this beautiful baby and who was taken from me at my most vulnerable age. Suddenly, I felt a terrible need for her – a need to have someone to share this joy with. David, who was named after my mother, Dvorah, became the focus of my life – my whole world and needless to say, his father's pride

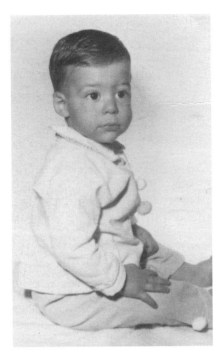

*David was born
September 9, 1958*

and joy. I was determined to be the best, most protective and most caring mother in the whole world. Whatever I missed in my childhood, I was determined to give to my children and so it was.

Irwin's parents, Grandma Ruth and Grandpa Abe, helped out with babysitting and his sister Selma became the adoring Aunt Selly to David, and later to the rest of our family, as well as to our future grand-children. Michelle came along a few years later and David who was the sole prince for three and a half years had to share his special status with his baby sister. Needless to say, he was not very happy with this new change in his life. Eventually he accepted the fact that she was here to stay.

David – the pride and joy of his mother and father

Irwin worked for a toy company and with our new status – a family of two; we decided that we needed larger quarters. So, we bought a semi-attached house (three bedrooms) in Far Rockaway. This new residence near the beach (Atlantic Ocean) became our permanent as well as our vacation home – since we couldn't afford to send the children to camp as did many of our friends. A bungalow colony was out of the question as well. Davies Road became the

Irwin with David & Michelle

oasis for all the children in the neighborhood. Summers were spent playing ball in the street and making sand castles on the beach. To this day, our children have the fondest memories of those summers spent doing "nothing."

One year we actually packed up the kids – David was eight and Michelle was four and a half – and set out on a three week adventure by car from New York to California. It was the only kind of vacation we could afford. We drove 500 miles a day, ate all our meals on the road (picnic style) and slept in

motels. By the time we reached Las Vegas, we wanted to spend an evening in the casino to try our luck at some slot machines. We had to leave the children in the room since it was against the law to bring children into a casino. David, we found out years later had visions of getting rid of his little pain in the neck sister once and for all – like throwing her out of the window without anyone ever being the wiser. We rarely left them alone after that.

Throughout the years, I continued to correspond with my father and my Aunt Miriam, his wife. There was no thought of ever meeting him again.

I was now 26 years old, married to a husband that my father had never met and two children (his grand-children) that he never saw. No one traveled to Israel in those years (1960s). Suddenly, one day I received a phone call from my Aunt Eva (my father's sister) telling me that my father was about to come to visit us in the United States. We were all in shock. The year was 1963 – Irwin suddenly had a father-in-law and he was about to meet him. I couldn't imagine what I would do with this "stranger" in my home for six weeks. I felt nothing for this man. In fact, I hardly remembered him.

The day came, and we set out for the airport. I pulled out a picture of my father so that we could recognize this man that was about to arrive.

While standing at the arrivals gate at JFK airport, two ladies standing next to me struck up a conversation with me. One of them told me that they were waiting for their sister to arrive from Israel, whom they hadn't seen in four years. The other one asked me whom I was waiting for. Suddenly, tears welled up in my eyes and I could hardly get the sentence out. "I'm waiting for my father and I haven't seen him in sixteen and a half years. The last time I saw him I was ten years old.

We all stood there in disbelief and as the tears flowed, I couldn't understand why I was overcome with such emotion. I suddenly felt sooo sorry for myself. I couldn't understand these mixed emotions since my father, whom I longed for as a child, was a total stranger to me now.

As the passengers started coming out, I looked for a tall thin man. I didn't see anyone fitting that description. Suddenly I saw this small man approaching us and I turned to my husband who was holding up this picture of my father – but this man approaching us didn't fit the description of a tall, thin man. Was it possible that this could be him? Could this man be my father? I asked this "stranger" in Yiddish "*Ir zent Muehlbauer?*" And he answered "*Yo*" – Yes. I cannot describe the feeling that came over me in that instant. There I was, "a child" again, and standing before me was my father.

All the years of separation and estrangement were forgotten. All I knew was that I loved this man and all the love came pouring out – in one instant no feelings turned into feelings of such deep emotion. We embraced and I knew I never wanted to be separated from him again. He was exactly how I had remembered him, except that when I was ten and little, he was much taller. He asked me if they had no food in America because I was so thin. His sense of humor was still there. As we became more acquainted, I asked him what made him come now. He said he felt a tremendous need to see me, see to whom I'm married, how I'm doing and of course to meet his grandchildren.

Irwin, I, and Father

When I asked him why he didn't come to my wedding on December 22, 1956, he told me that this was the Sinai Campaign between Israel and Egypt and the borders were closed and travel in and out of Israel at that time was forbidden. Years later, I learned from one of my father's close friends how frustrated and miserable my father was on that day knowing that his only child was getting married and he couldn't be there to share that special time with her. Of course, I didn't know any of this at the time. I also didn't know how much my father suffered in his own way through all these years of separation.

At one point, I saw my father standing over his wedding picture (his and my mother's) that was hanging on my bedroom wall – tears welled up in his eyes – I could only guess what could possibly be going on in his mind. His youth? The destruction that Hitler had wrought on all of us? The dead and the living?

My father never spoke about his past, much to my

Father, Irwin, David, and Michelle –
summer 1963

sorrow, and I never questioned him. I didn't want to bring any more pain to his life. Today I realize that this was a great mistake for I know nothing of my mother (*zt'l*) – who she was, what she was like, etc. etc. I can't ever repair this void in my heart now. That part of my heart will always remain empty.

The summer passed quickly and the only way my father would leave our home and his newfound family

Cousin Walter, Father, Aunt Gladys, and Uncle Sam Silverman

and go back to Israel was with a promise that we would soon come to visit him in Israel.

Now that was not so easy for us in those years, 1963 and on, travel to Israel was rare and very expensive, especially for a young couple with two small children. But a promise is a promise, and our desire to see each other again became an obsession – a dream. All I could think of was the moment when I would see my father again.

Our family's needs were the same as any growing family, but we did without a lot of extras and tried to save every penny toward our goal.

Years later – Mom Ruthie with Daniella

Chapter Five

Our Trips To Israel

Our first visit to Israel took place in 1965. I can't explain the feeling that came over me the minute I saw this great big jet with a blue and white star of David on it. It was the most unbelievable sight – a Jewish airline – El Al. When we finally landed in Israel and the Hebrew tape came over the intercom playing "*Heiveinu Shalom Aleichem,*" I started to cry. The realization that I was actually in Israel – stepping on Israeli soil, a free Jewish country after what Hitler did to us, was too much for me to bear. Hitler tried to wipe every Jew off the face of the earth and here we were – a proud Jewish nation. But this tiny country paid a very heavy price for its freedom.

The War of Independence in 1948 was fought against all odds and won by the sheer will and sacrifice of its people. Then came the Sinai Campaign in 1956 between Israel and

The El Al Airplane

Egypt. And now a new threat was looming on the horizon.

The people we met during our first visit were all talking about the Arab aggression and the upcoming war to destroy Israel. Life in this tiny country of milk and honey was beautiful but it was fraught with danger. Young fathers with small children were talking about having to take up arms again because the Arabs wouldn't let them live in peace. This was the reality of life in Israel in the summer of 1965.

We enjoyed a beautiful visit with our family. My father, Aunt Miriam, my cousins Ciporah and Nachum Avtalion and their and our children. We traveled throughout the country and were amazed at the contrast between the modern and the Biblical sights. We became instantly Zionized. I wanted to remain in Israel and never go back to America. I felt that this was the only place for a Jew to live.

I especially felt guilty that we, as Jews, were enjoying this beautiful land but didn't share in its burdens. This has remained my feeling throughout my entire life till today.

We also

From right to left:
Father, Rivka Meytal, Ciporah and I.
Bottom row children: Amir Meytal, Ceela Avtalion, Michelle, and David, 1965

met some wonderful friends that have remained close to us throughout the years. One such couple in particular is David and Rivka Meytal.

They had two small children our children's age and they all played to-

Father and Aunt Miriam

gether that whole summer. Their son Amir was five, a year younger than our David who was six at the time. And their daughter Michal was about two, the same as our Michelle. Their father was a truck driver and he would take the children for rides on his truck. We spent

Friends we met on our first trip to Israel:
Ciporah and Nachman, Rivka and David,
Sara and Ariel Meytal, Irwin and I – Summer 1965

Friends: Amir Meytal & David Weber

beautiful days swimming in the Mediterranean Sea and the children played and built castles in the sand. These were the best of times and we thought they would last forever.

When it was time for us to go home everyone was teary eyed, but promised to write to each other and to come back as soon as possible.

When we returned to the United States, I decided to start studying Hebrew. I needed to be able to speak the language that I knew I'd be using in the future and I had the feeling that there would come a day in my life when I would be very connected to this land and so it was.

Zeide Abe with Michelle and David

Time passed and the situation between the Arabs and Israel worsened to the point that war became imminent. I wrote to my family and to our friends that they should consider sending their children to the U.S. for safety. The whole country was mobilized – but they never thought of sending their children to us. This after all, was not Europe and not the Holocaust. This was a free and independent Israel.

The year was 1967 – we never dreamed that such a miracle would occur and that little Israel would defeat all the strong Arab armies and in only six days. And to culminate the Arab's great defeat, to reunify Jerusalem, the world could not believe that little Israel achieved such a great victory. Little David slew Goliath.

Everyone was suddenly proud to be a Jew. Jews were the heroes of the world and Israel became a very popular tourist attraction. This was a historical moment and we wanted to be a part of it. We packed our kids, our bags, and off we went – it was July 1967, a few weeks after the "Six Day" war ended.

Our children resumed their relationship with their cousins and their friends and Amir Meytal and David Weber became even closer friends. We made many trips throughout the country together. We visited Kibbutzim and the Galil, the Kineret and the Golan Heights and of course the reunited capital Jerusalem – the Western Wall and all the places that were newly captured in the war – a war that was started by the Arabs and defeated by the proud Israeli Army.

Amir's father, David who was still driving a truck

Irwin and I in front of some antiquities in the ancient city of Caessarea. (This building later housed the famous Caessarea Art Gallery, owned and managed by David Meytal)

was privately dabbling in art. It was a hobby that he never thought would develop into anything more than that. One day, he asked me to look at some of his paintings which I considered quite good. He was thirty-five at the time. I encouraged him to start taking some courses in art and to pursue his talent. This gave him the impetus to register in an art school in Tel Aviv. The rest is history.

David Meytal is today a prominent artist. Not only did David Meytal become an artist, but because of his knowledge of art history, the city council of Caessarea gave him permission to open an art gallery on an archeological site which became one of Israel's top tourist attractions. To this day, he remains grateful for this encouragement. The talent was there. All that he needed was a "push" to develop it and I couldn't be more proud of the end results. Today his monumental canvases decorate the walls of many public places throughout Israel. In turn, I learned a great deal about art from him and years later became an art dealer myself.

David sponsored some talented Israeli artists and sent them to the U.S. to further their careers – with my help and promotion, some of them became quite successful. I worked with one artist in particular – his name is Avi Adler. Today his work can be seen in the Jerusalem Museum, the Jewish Museum in New York, as well as some prominent galleries here and abroad.

Our third child Debbie – Dvorah (also named for my mother (*zt'l*), was born April 2, 1969. Three months later we were on our way to Israel again – this time to show the new baby to our family and friends. My father became the babysitter once again and he couldn't have

Father with baby Debbie, 1969

On tour in Jerusalem

been happier. We lived in his house, but this time it was becoming a little crowded so we decided to buy an apartment of our own nearby. We were very fortunate that our cousins Nachman and Ciporah offered to look after the apartment for us while we went back home to the U.S. In Israel, we had our privacy and we became citizens of Hadera, our new second home.

Nachman, Ciporah, and I

As the years passed and our visits became more frequent, we got more and more involved in Israeli social life. We became part of the "chevra" in Hadera.

When we returned to the U.S., we threw a big Kiddush in honor of the birth of our new baby girl, Debbie. We invited a young Israeli couple to the Kiddush. They were both teachers on Sabbatical from Israel, living and working in New York. Itzhak and Arella Naor became our friends in the fall of 1969 and have remained part of our family since then till today.

Our next trip to Israel was in the summer of 1971, the year that our son David put on his Tefillin at the Kotel (the Western Wall). This was and remains a most memorable moment in all our lives. Our friends and family shared this beautiful simcha with us.

When we came back home to the U.S., we had another Bar Mitzvah celebration. David said his Haftorah beautifully, watched over by his wonderful and devoted teacher, Norman Rosenman. How can I describe the

At the Kotel, 1971

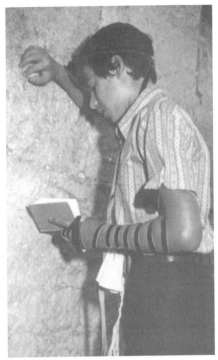

David puts on his tefillin

Father with Debbie

Family and friends

Proud Mom and Dad with David

pride and joy that Irwin and I felt that Shabbat morning watching our little boy become a man? One must cherish these special moments for they come only once in a lifetime – if you're lucky. We had the zechut to enjoy

Proud sisters
Debbie and Michelle with David

that moment. The big Gala came the next day on Sunday in the White Shul attended by Grandpa Abe and Mom Ruthie, Aunt Selly, friends and family and of course sisters, Michelle and Debbie and all of David's friends as well. It was a beautiful party – the first of many more to come.

1973 brought to Israel another war – the Yom Kippur war. Israel was attacked on the holiest day of the year. The country had to quickly mobilize – men were taken out of synagogues to join their fighting units. Israel again miraculously won this war at the expense of thousands of casualties. The brave general who turned the course of the war around was General Ariel Sharon. As with any great leader, he was revered and he was cursed by some. But because of his leadership, Israel survived and miraculously won the war.

I'm with Golda Meir on the 25th anniversary of Israel in Caessarea

Some years later, Irwin and I were called upon to host General Sharon in our home. He had retired from the Army and was entering politics. He was interested in meeting American Jews to support his new political party – Shlomzion. This was April of 1977. Because of our affiliation with Israel and our Zionist approach, we were asked to host a parlor meeting for him. Many people were against him at the time and were critical of us for agreeing to do this. But, all I could think of was this man's greatness and dedication to Israel and her survival, so I knew

Irwin and myself with General Sharon

Irwin with General Sharon in our home

that it was important for us to do whatever was in our power to help and give him encouragement in his political quest. No one had confidence in him that he would attain a position in politics. Well, as became obvious in the following years, they were all wrong and we

GENERAL ARIEL SHARON

SHLOMZION
4 Haarba Street
Tel Aviv, Israel

May 6, 1977

Mr. & Mrs. Irwin Weber
7 Boxwood Lane
Lawrence, N.Y. 11559

Dear Esther & Irwin:

I would like to personally thank you for arranging
for me to speak in your home in New York. Your warmth and
hospitality really meant a lot to me during these very tough
days.

Thank you also your your very, very generous contribution
to the SHLOMZION Party.

Because you are a friend and an American supporter of
my candidacy, I thought you would be interested in the enclosed
item from the New York Times.

Our party is now waging a vigorous campaign in what many
say is the most important election in Israel's history. You
have been most generous to me and I want you to know how much
I deeply appreciate your support.

I look forward to meeting with you again in Israel on
your next visit.

Sincerely,

A. Sharon

Amir at Pnimia in Haifa

were right. He became Prime Minister of Israel and one of her great leaders and the rest is history.

The years passed and on our next trip to Israel, we were invited to attend a ceremony at a military school in Haifa. This was a school for children 13 years old and Amir Meytal was one of the students. This was the beginning of Amir's military career. He was still a child but his future was already being carved out for him.

Amir, Irwin, and Debbie

And what a proud and glorious future he would have. We attended his graduation as well as his first parachute jump.

By the time the Lebanese War broke out, he was

Amir played with the baby

a full fledged soldier – a Golani soldier – he had graduated to a special forces unit – the Sayeret Golani – these soldiers were amongst the best fighters in the army – and Amir was the best of the best. Our son David was proud to call Amir his friend. To Irwin and me, Amir was another son.

David, Daniella, and Amir

Amir and Michelle

Through the years, we watched these two boys grow. One in Israel, one in America – there were years that our David was taller than Amir and then Amir suddenly shot up and caught up to David in height. David got married to Aviva Stavish and Amir was still in the army. David and Aviva had their first child,

Rivka, Rivi, Amir, and I

Daniella and on a visit to Israel that year, Amir played

with the baby.

David and Amir remained friends. Whenever we were in Israel, Amir would always try to see us no matter how busy he was.

One time, he was on his way to Lebanon with a whole convoy of tanks following his lead. He took a detour past our house just to say good-bye to us. I couldn't believe what he had done. When I asked him why he took the time to pass by, his answer was – when was I going to see you again – you were going back to America and I was off to Lebanon and I had to say good-bye. This was Amir Meytal.

Michelle, Yirmie Sharabi, Amir, and I

Chapter Six

Purpose To My Survival

The summer of the Lebanese War (1982), Irwin and I were called to volunteer at Tel Hashomer Hospital in Tel Aviv. There we met many wounded soldiers that were the age of our son. These boys had lost legs, arms, and all I could think of was what help we could give them to overcome their terrible plight.

We came upon the idea that to give them some encouragement to go on, we would arrange a trip for them to visit the U.S. They all laughed and thought we were crazy. They never believed we would go through with this plan. When Amir heard this, he was very proud – to him and to us, there was no one more holy than the Israeli soldier.

Months passed and we sent our daughter Michelle to make all the arrangements for the trip. She got them their passports, visas, tickets, etc. and the day came when we went to the airport to meet and greet them and bring them to our home.

We spent three exhausting and exhilarating weeks together. But these were the most memorable weeks of our lives. These boys came to us as invalids and went back home like tourists – loaded down with cameras, newfound friendships, and many fond memories as well as wonderful experiences.

Permit me to give you a little background on some of these young heroes.

One, Yirmie Sharabi was hit by a rocket while trapped in his tank – he lost his leg, but in order to save his life, he went through ten operations each time cutting off a little more of his limb. He was so depressed, he wanted to kill himself, but because of this trip and the encouragement of his fellow comrades, he was prodded into using his prosthesis. By the time he returned to Israel, he walked on both feet, with the help of his prosthesis. When I went to visit his parents on my next trip, they fell on the floor and kissed my hands and feet and told me that I had returned their son from a state of vegetation to a human being. Today Yirmie is well, productive, and a happily married man.

Another one was Ori Tzarfati, who when he was wounded with five bullets in his chest and taken to Rambam Hospital in Haifa, his sister, who was a nurse there, was called in to take care of a soldier being brought in by medical helicopter – she didn't know it was her brother. Before they could even look at Ori's shattered leg, they (the surgeons) had to stop the bleeding in his chest to save his life. They later amputated his leg. He is today completely rehabilitated – wind surfing, motor biking, married with two daughters.

Then there is Michael Katzenelson (Katza for short). He lost his leg below the knee but it didn't shatter his psyche. When we first met him at the hospital, his face was totally black. I said to my husband, what a

Group: Ori, Shlomo, Tomer, Eitie, Katza, Uri, and Debbie

pity that this poor young man has to live with such a terrible burden. But, day after day, his face started to get lighter and lighter. What we didn't know at our original meeting was that his whole face was covered by shrapnel and little by little, the shrapnel came to the surface. Today he's a handsome young man with a clean face, an Olympic swimmer, at the Beit Halochem Rehabilitation Center in Tel Aviv and a happily married man.

Shlomo Trabulsi, from Tzefat, has his own interesting story which I would like to share with you as well. He was wounded in his leg by "friendly fire." The Israeli Army, in its rush to get at the enemy, unfortunately fired on some of its own troops by mistake. Sadly, Shlomo was one of these casualties. When he was taken

Moshe, Shlomo, and Ori

to the hospital and brought into the surgical ward, he did not give permission to have his leg amputated. Because he was in fear of losing his leg, each time he was examined by the doctors, he lied and told them he was okay, when in truth, he was in constant pain. They provided a "brace" for his leg which he still wears today.

The law in the Defense Ministry of Israel is that you receive certain benefits according to your disability. Originally, Shlomo's disability was designated around 65% but as he wasn't complaining and kept telling the doctors that he "felt fine," they lowered his disability to below 50%. So he was not entitled to some of the benefits such as a car (specially equipped) that the other boys got. As time passed, living in Tzefat, which is located in the northern part of Israel, where it gets pretty cold, he began to suffer more and more and it was very difficult for him to get around. He called us up and told us his story for he had no one else to turn to.

Because I was so involved in raising funds for "Beit Halochem," the rehabilitation center for wounded Israeli soldiers, I was very well known in Israel and had some pull. I called the Defense Minister and explained Shlomo's plight to him and lo and behold, we changed his medical status to "over 50%" disability and he was told that he would be getting a car. He learned how to drive, and in the end, this became his livelihood. He is today a taxi driver in Tzefat and a happily married man with a beautiful family. To this day, he still wonders how suddenly his status changed and he received a specially equipped car. This remains our little secret.

Recently one of our children's friends was visiting in Israel and they happened to get into a taxi in Tzefat. They struck up a conversation with the driver. The driver asked them if they happen to know a family Weber, and then he proceeded to tell them his whole story and how proud he was to part of "our family," and how the trip to the U.S. had changed his life.

Uvi Ben Chaim was another one of "our boys," whose life was changed by the trip. He was hit by a bullet that entered one side of his temple and went out the other side. He was totally paralyzed when we met him. This was after he had undergone a ten-hour brain operation.

After months of physical therapy, he began to regain some of his feelings and was able to walk again. He made the trip with the rest of the group and showed us all what a brave and courageous young man he was.

Along the road to recover

Uvi Ben Haim: *cheerful most of the time.*   Aliza Auerbach

Published weekly • June 12-18, 1983

WE MET UVI, still excited about his American trip, in his mother's Bat Yam apartment. He and five other war-wounded (one accompanied by his wife) had been invited to New York by Erwin and Esther Webber, whose daughter had got to know the boys while working as a volunteer at Tel Hashomer. The Webbers had put all seven of them up in their Long Island home and taken them everywhere from Washington to Niagara Falls.

"Wonderful people," enthused Uvi. "You should write about them and all they did for us — not about me."

The good-looking Uvi, who insisted on combing his hair before being photographed, walks better than he did, but still with an awkward lurch. He hasn't stopped suffering from headaches and takes pain killers on a regular basis. His memory is erratic and he has been forced to learn mathematics from scratch. He has not been able to learn to swim again since his injury and this depresses him, although most of the time he is cheerful.

Once he fell for no apparent reason and had to be hospitalized for several weeks. This is his main fear: that it will happen again. He cannot work at his former trade, carpentry. "I get sudden cramps," he explains. "It would be dangerous to get a cramp while I was working with a band-saw. His plan to open a furniture shop is still operational and he is undergoing aptitude tests, which he hopes will result in approval for the scheme and assistance from the Defence Ministry.

Most of his efforts recently were directed towards finding an apartment. It had to be on the ground floor, he explained, because steps were still a problem. Eventually he found a place just down the road from his mother. The ministry pays $300 a month towards the rent and he has to add another $20 himself. He has his disability pension; he is considered 100 per cent-plus disabled. His Volvo was purchased with a special loan and without taxes; but he had to fight for everything, he says.

"They give it to you eventually, but you have to stand up for your rights," he said, noting that the payment for the rent was not updated to the current exchange-rate, so he had to make another claim for the balance.

After making us coffee in his mother's home, Uvi insisted on driving us to his own flat. His car is adapted for driving with hands only, but I noticed he used his leg to brake. He experiments with using the right leg, he told me. The problem is that he doesn't have feeling in the foot.

He proudly showed us around his flat, which is roomy and pleasant, decorated with his own wood carvings. He likes biblical motifs: Samson and the pillars, Moses and the tablets, Adam and Eve.

His army officers and comrades have kept in touch. The evening we saw him he was planning to drive up to Jerusalem to the wedding of one of his former company commanders. "He told me that he wants to see me dancing at his wedding," laughed Uvi, looking forward to seeing all the boys again.

THE JERUSALEM POST INTERNATIONAL EDITION

Group photo at the Capitol in Washington, D.C.

Throughout the trip, they never once complained. When I would ask them how they felt, their answer was always "What, are we sick? We're soldiers and soldiers are strong." And that they were.

There was also Tomer and his wife who accompanied her husband and was somewhat a help to me. Tomer was the spokesman for the group as he was a teacher by profession and his English was impeccable. We had some very interesting meetings with high school kids in the area, HAFTR in particular.

These kids were very anxious to meet these Israeli heroes.

One of our excursions took us to Washington D.C. We joined a trip with HAFTR High School. It was a

THURSDAY, MAY 12, 1983 **HAFTR Hosts Israeli War Heroes**

The 8th graders were involved in a unique experience which has greatly affected t[ ]
lives. Through the efforts of Yeshiva parents, Esther and Irwin Weber of Lawrence,
Israeli soldiers, badly wounded in the Lebanese War, were treated to their first tou[ ]
the United States and were soon "adopted" by the HAFTR student body.

At Rabbi Rosner's invitation, the group joined the 8th graders for a three day tou[ ]
Washington, D.C. In addition to the traditional touring of the nation's capital and a[ ]
sonal meeting with Senator Al D'Amato, the group participated in the opening ceremon[ ]
the American Holocaust Survivors Conference and was privileged to hear such notable[ ]
President Reagan, Elie Wiesel and Chief Rabbi Lau of Netanya, Israel.

Throughout the trip, the young soldiers (five of the six are barely out of their tee[ ]
most of whom are amputees, captivated the students with their personal, heart—warming[ ]
ries and with their total dedication to their homeland. This special relationship bet[ ]
the students and the soldiers was reinforced further at the school's celebration on Is[ ]
Independence Day, where they sang and danced joyously together.

As the soldiers returned home after spending three weeks as guests of the Webers,[ ]
who had been in contact with them agreed that their infectious enthusiasm and sense of[ ]
pose had left an indelible impression of inspiration to all.

THURSDAY, MAY 12, 1983 **NASSAU HERALD**

THURSDAY, MAY 12, 1983 **NASSAU HERALD**

three-day bus trip and the kids all wanted the soldiers to be on their bus. One of the high school graduates, that year's valedictorian, spoke about the special privilege it was to have met and spent time with these true Israeli heroes and how they would never forget it.

One funny experience that I would like to share with you, that happened in Washington DC, was an evening excursion to the Washington Memorial (The Obelisk). The guys wanted to see the view of Washington from the top, but there was a very long line to get to the elevators. So, I went to the front of the line to speak to the park ranger. I told him I had a group of Israeli wounded Vets that couldn't stand on such a long line. With that the ranger took off his "Smokey the Bear" hat and showed me that he was wearing a yarmulke and said, "Israeli soldiers, I am Jewish

Park Ranger and I

too. Let's go." And up to the top we went, bypassing the entire line. The park ranger then promised to visit them all in Israel.

One Shabbat, we all went to The White Shul (Knesseth Israel). It was a rainy day and the walk was very difficult since the rain got into their prostheses and made it even heavier and more difficult to walk. But in the end we made it and when it was time to introduce them to the congregation, Rabbi Pelcovitz introduced them and gave his whole Dvar Torah in Hebrew so that the boys could understand him. He then called each one of them up to the Bima for an *Aliyah LeTorah*.

These boys who stopped bullets with their own bodies, who were crippled in bodies but not in their souls, were honored on that Shabbat morning and there wasn't a dry eye in the audience. Till today, people come up to me and tell me that they will never forget that "special" Shabbat.

One day, I received a phone call from a gentleman in Brooklyn. Somehow, he found out about this Israeli group visiting in the U.S. and asked me if he could arrange to take them out for an evening of theater and dinner. I was very happy to accept the offer.

The day arrived and three cars pulled up in front of my house. When I went out to greet them, I found out that they themselves were veterans of World War II who were all "double" amputees. They came with their wives to meet and greet these young men who were amputees as well, and to show them that they could live a normal life – get married, have a family, etc. etc. It was a very special and meaningful evening for all of us.

This entire project succeeded beyond our wildest expectations. We gained a lot more than we gave. We will never forget these heartwarming experiences.

By the time they had to leave, we had to promise that we would soon come and visit them in their homes in Israel and so we did. We went to each wedding and at each wedding we had the honor of standing next to

Going home – Kennedy Airport

their parents under the Chupah. We were and are today one big happy family. Each time a new baby is born, we become grandparents once again. Whenever we're in Israel, we arrange a reunion between all of them. They look forward to our trips, as do we to seeing all of them once again.

Because of our close connection to Israel, we met some of the most wonderful people with whom we've remained close through the years. One such couple in particular is Buky and Sarit Oren. They came into our lives about sixteen years ago because of their beautiful little boy Almog, who at that time was stricken with cancer in both of his eyes. Irwin and I were called upon to help them through this very difficult period in their life. Their bravery and courage in dealing with this insurmountable problem taught us all a lesson in life. Unfortunately, all their monumental efforts didn't succeed in saving Almog's life. They lost Almog just before his thirteenth birthday, but our relationship with these wonderful and courageous people continues till today. Because of Almog's short but meaningful life on this earth we have all benefited and he will always remain a part of us.

Almog, with Irwin and I

ZAHAL DISABLED VETERANS
ORGANISATION

TEL – AVIV BRANCH

ארגון נכי צה״ל

סניף – תל־אביב

51, Chen Boulevard, P.O.Box 11161, Tel-Aviv 61111   Tel. (03)221286-7 .טל   שד׳ חן, 51, ת. ד. 11161 תל־אביב 61111

Our ref : .... : מספרנו   Tel-Aviv, The .... יום ,תל־אביב,

Dear Irwin and Esther Webber,

We were informed by the Zahal Disabled War Veterans, who were hospitalised in the Tel Hashomer Hospital, in the rehabilitation ward, that you were awarded the GUEST OF HONOUR in your community and we are honoured to acknowledge it. You certainly deserve it. We are all aware of your contribution and support in the care of the disabled war veterans and their rehabilitation.

This is to express our heartfelt appreciation for all you have both done and do.

We wish you both health and strength and many years more of blessed work, in the community and with the Zahal Disabled War Veterans.

Yours sincerely,

NACHUM GAMADY.

Years later, I was honored at our synagogue, The White Shul, as the "Woman of the Year – Eishet Chayil." I was asked to make a speech and didn't quite know what I would talk about. Suddenly it came to me.

For years, I wondered why I survived the terrible horror of the Holocaust when so many had perished. Perhaps there was a purpose to my survival. Perhaps I had a job to do. I realized that being there for these soldiers, and making a difference for Almog, with Irwin and I in their lives, this was a reason for my survival. Because there were people in my life who had helped me, I had to reach out to those who needed my help as well. I realized, in the end, that G-d did have a plan for me. He saved me for a reason – that reason has become more obvious to me with each passing year.

Eishet Chayil Dinner
Irwin and I, David, Michelle, and Debbie

As the years passed, I became more and more involved with organizational work – always for the benefit of disabled veterans. One year, with the help of the Bnei Zion organization, I decided that we could do a great fundraiser for the Soldiers Fund on Yom Haatzmaut – Israel's Independence Day. This was going to be the biggest event New York had ever done for the benefit of Beit Halochem (another name for the House of the Warriors). All the proceeds from the event were going to benefit the rehabilitation center.

We chose to do this on the "U.S.S. Intrepid," a famous battleship from World War II. This was going to serve a dual purpose – to promote the Intrepid as a museum and to raise awareness for Beit Halochem – the soldier's fund. This gala affair drew over 4,000 supporters onto the air force carrier for an evening of fun and celebrations. There was entertainment, food, dancing, topped off with the famous Garucci Fireworks that lit up the entire New York Harbor. It was a happening and a source of great satisfaction for all who participated. No one has ever forgotten that beautiful event.

Some years later, Ellis Island opened to the public. When I went to visit the place where I had first landed over fifty years ago, it brought back some long forgotten memories. There were forms to be filled out for anyone who had participated in the history of Ellis Island. I filled out a form stating that I had arrived and was processed on the island in 1948. I later received a phone call from an agent of the Federal Government asking if I would care to give a deposition for their historical archives. I agreed to do this and it became one of the many thousand stories of immigrants arriving on these shores. It is there as a public record.

Some time passed and I was notified that a theater on West 46th Street was showing a special production called "Coming Through." This play was about immigration and one of the stories chosen was "my story" – the story of my arrival to the U.S., via Ellis Island. Naturally, I was curious to see the play. When I met the actress that played the role of Esther Muhlbauer, I was amazed how accurately the director had chosen someone who almost looked like me fifty years later.

When I purchased my ticket, and announced my name, everyone became very excited. The actress Ellen Evans told me she would be too flustered to play me now that I would be in the audience. It was all very funny – especially when the director came over to me

Actress Ellen Evans and I

and asked me if he could introduce me after the show and if I would come up on stage and say a few words.

When I accepted to do it, my husband and children who were with me could not believe that I would actually get on stage and speak in front of this large audience without any previous preparation.

Well, speak I did and in the end, got a standing ovation for my effort. My family expected to be very

Standing on stage of "Coming Through"

embarrassed but in the end, they were very proud.

What I chose to speak about was my return trip to Poland, my coming to America, and my general philosophy about life and what you can do with it. I spoke about the opportunities that America had offered me and that with a little education and hard work and the right attitude, there wasn't a thing you couldn't achieve in this wonderful land of opportunity. And I meant every word of it.

THE ARTS

Wynn Handman, center, with the cast of "Coming Through," clockwise from right, Mara Stevens, Thomas Pennacchini, Shawn McNesby, David Kener and David Warren.

Photo by Vicky Kasala

The Immigrant Experience

"Coming Through," an interactive drama drawn from the rich oral histories of immigrants who passed through Ellis Island in the early 1920s, is playing at the American Place Theater, 111 W. 46th St., Manhattan.

Directed by Wynn Handman, the play celebrates the experience of the uprooted men and women who came to create new lives in America. The script was adapted by Handman from the testimonies of immigrants collected by the Ellis Island Oral History Project.

The five-member cast joins with the audience to savor the resilience, ingenuity and survival of these immigrants, and bring theatrical life to their evocative and compelling experiences.

United States Department of the Interior

NATIONAL PARK SERVICE
Statue of Liberty National Monument
Liberty Island
New York, New York 10004

IN REPLY REFER TO:

February 25, 1995

Dear Irwin;

I met your wife Esther when I came to interview her for the Ellis Island Immigration Museum's Oral History Project. At this time of a testimonial to her and to you I am struck by a vow that she told me she made to herself after her arrival in this country in 1948. At the time she was a child alone, being shunted between extended family members who were themselves struggling. She remembered in my interview with her that she had said to herself, "I'm going to grow up and I'm going to make something of myself. And I'm going to prove to the whole world that I'm worthy of surviving."

Esther, as you know, was three years old when her parents left her with Christian friends, thus beginning the horrors that she experienced in Poland. I think of her much like the beautiful child in the rose colored coat and hat in the film Schindler's List. She represents life.

Her story is a Jewish story. The horrific experiences of the Holocaust have effects on people the variety of which is as great as there is variety in personalities. Esther, who has undergone so much and has gone on to help and encourage others in so many ways, has, in deed, proved to the whole world that she has grown up, she has made something of herself, and indeed is worthy of being called a beautiful human being.

I am very happy to have met her and I send my heart-felt congratulations to you both.

Yours truly,

Janet Levine

Janet Levine, Ph.D.
Oral Historian

Chapter Seven

Finding My Roots

A few years ago, June 8, 1993, to be exact, our daughter Debbie and her husband Michael Schreiber decided that they were going to make a trip to Eastern Europe – a Jewish heritage trip. One evening they sat us down and asked Irwin and me to join them on this trip. First, we were in shock. I never thought about going back to Poland and this was the last place that Irwin thought to visit. We were in a quandary.

Michael's words to us were "Deb and I are going anyway, but it would be more meaningful for us if you would join us." Well, with this in mind, we began to give the idea some consideration. The more I thought about it, the more I realized that if I were ever to return to Poland this would be the incentive. But, I was also afraid of facing what I might face. I knew who I was today. How would I feel after such a trip? It was a chance that I decided I must take. Irwin went along with my decision. As always, he was supportive of whatever I would decide.

I didn't know what I could accomplish on this trip but one thing I knew I had to do was to go to the town where my mother was taken off the train and murdered in cold blood. If I could accomplish this, then the trip would be worth my while. I also thought about trying to find the town where I was left by my father and to see if I could find any member of the Bik family.

The problem was that the town didn't exist on any map that I could find. I inquired at the Polish Embassy and they had no record of Krzemienica, so we decided that we would hire a private car with a driver and see what we could find. That was the only plan we had when we left the States.

Our journey led us to Czechoslovakia, Hungary (Budapest), Brataslavia and finally to Warsaw. When we arrived in Warsaw, we stayed at the Forum Hotel for one Shabbat. When we arrived in Poland, I couldn't contain my excitement. One thing I wanted to prove to myself was that there was a "Black Forest" in Warsaw and it was near some railroad tracks. I remembered this from my childhood. I needed to prove to myself that this was really where I was and not some childhood dream. I asked the concierge at the hotel if there was a forest anywhere in Warsaw. Sure enough, he pointed it out on the city map and told me it was about fifteen minutes drive from the hotel. At eleven o'clock at night, I had a taxi drive us deep into the forest just to prove to me that it really existed.

That Shabbat we went to the main synagogue and all I could think of was what a miracle all this was – the fact that the last time I was in this place, we were hunted like dogs and today we were here as free Jews. To see my husband and my son-in-law Michael praying with a minyan in a synagogue in Warsaw was for me a sight that brought tears to my eyes. That I survived the horrors of this war, got married and lived to have a wonderful daughter Debbie and her husband Michael pray with me in this synagogue was too much to bear. But who's to question all of G-d's miracles.

Next to Michael stood a young man who didn't even look Jewish. When Michael asked him about his background, he explained that he was Jewish but was brought up totally assimilated. His dream was to someday go to Israel, meet a Jewish girl, and live a Jewish life. His problem was that he was about to be drafted into the Polish Army and he had no one to turn to help him get to Israel.

With that, our son-in-law Michael told him to come to our hotel after Shabbat and we would try to help him somehow.

Gregory arrived at our hotel as scheduled and he explained his dilemma to us. What he needed was an invitation from someone in Israel such as a Kibbutz and with this invitation, he could go to the Israeli Embassy in Poland and perhaps get a visa to leave. We called some of our connections in Israel and asked them to help us get this young man out of Poland. They promised to do whatever they could and with this information, we bid Gregory good-bye.

We were in Warsaw only 48 hours, but it was as if we were meant to be there – a few weeks later we received a fax from Gregory – "Thanks to you, I am on my way to Israel." Several years later, we found Gregory studying in a Yeshiva in Jerusalem. His name was now "Moshe" and he was happily reunited with his parents who by now accepted his desire to live a Jewish life in a Jewish land.

Gregory and I in Jerusalem

From Warsaw, our journey continued to Krakow and to Auschwitz (Oshvietzin in Polish), then to Birkenau – the camps, the gas chambers, the grounds that were soaked in blood. We passed through the gates that read "Arbeit Macht Frei – Work means freedom" – what an insult – what a sadistic joke – when all the Germans wanted to do was bring every Jewish man, woman and child by cattle cars to their final destination – the gas chambers.

Debbie and I at Auschwitz

When we returned to our hotel in Krakow we met our

Michael, Debbie, Irwin, and I at Depica train station

Irwin saying Kaddish for my mother at the train station

prearranged taxi driver and started on our next journey.

It was five p.m. and the first place I wanted to go to was the town called Dembitza. This was where my mother (*zt'l*), was taken off the train and shot in cold blood. When we got to this town, there wasn't a monument or any acknowledgment of the thousands of

Irwin, Michael, Debbie, and I

Jews that were killed here. So we went to the train station, my mother's last resting place. There my husband and son-in-law said Kaddish and my daughter Debbie and I stood silently and said our own personal prayers. If for no other reason than to be here at this train station, the last stop and my mother's burial place to find some closure to my life, then the trip to Poland was worth the effort.

When Michael and Debbie had first proposed the trip, they had no idea how true their words would be "Mom, Dad it will be more meaningful for us if you join us on this trip to Poland and Eastern Europe." How right they were. In the end, it was the most meaningful trip for me and for Irwin as well.

After we left the town of Dembitza, we started driving toward the town of Mielitz. I had not given up on the idea of finding the Bik Family. Though the driver was very discouraging and it was getting late in the evening, he actually told us that people spent weeks trying to find a place that isn't even on a map so how did I expect to find anyone in one evening? But, I was determined and with some information that my father had provided we continued.

When we arrived in this one town Mielitz, I knew that we were not too far from Krzemienica – only about fifteen kilometers. We asked an elderly man for some directions and if he knew which way was to Krzemienica. Sure enough, he showed us which road to take.

I found Krzemienica!

After driving a few kilometers, we suddenly came upon a sign Krzemienica. At that point, I started directing the driver where to turn off. The last time I was here, I was three years old, but I knew exactly where to go. I told the driver to stop at a certain farmhouse. I said, "This is it. Stop right here." Everyone thought I was crazy. Just then, I saw a young man standing in front of a picket fence.

I jumped out of the car, needless to say, very excited and I asked him in Polish if he knew a family "Bik." That's when he pointed to himself and said, "I Bik." I turned to the driver and to my family who were standing there in amazement. No one could believe that I could possibly have remembered all this, fifty years later. My daughter Debbie started to cry. I almost fainted from excitement. Michael's next words were "Spielberg, you have nothing on us. This is the real thing."

I asked this young man about Joseph Bik and he told me that Joseph Bik was his uncle but he wasn't alive anymore. "But the brother of Joseph Bik is my father."

By now, it was nine o'clock in the evening, pitch dark, dogs were barking, cows were mooing and here we were standing in the middle of a dirt road in front of an old farmhouse with only the lights from our car lighting us up. I asked this young man if he could call his father to come out to talk to us and he did.

The father was now a man of seventy-two years and I asked him if he ever heard of a family Muehlbauer, to which he replied, he knew a Chune Muehlbauer (my father) and a Chava Muehlbauer (my Aunt Eva) and Mashek Muehlbauer (my grandfather). Much to our amazement, he mentioned them all by their Hebrew names.

Then he told us that there was a child here that they were hiding but he didn't know whatever happened to her. With that, I showed him (pointing to myself) that I was that child and that I came back to try to find the family. They embraced me and asked us all to come in to the house where we sat talking till about one in the morning just reminiscing.

Everyone was talking and crying including the Polish driver. Who could ever believe that such a reunion could actually take place after fifty years and from the memory of a three-year-old child?

Stanislav Bik and I

The young man, whom we met at the gate, brought me flowers and kissed my hands and told me how grateful they all were that we came to visit them. He also explained to us that his father had told them the story about us but they never believed it till we showed up and proved him to be right. We are now in correspondence with the family and hope to register them in Jerusalem as "Righteous Gentiles."

A Letter From The Bik Family

My name is Stanislaw Bik (Stan).
I am the second son of Marian Bik, and
I am 45 years old.
 My family ask me to write to you, because
they don't know English, as you know.
My English isn't perfect too, but I will
try to write a little bit about our family.
 Huno's father was friend a my grandfather
Wojciech Bik, he had four children.
The oldest one is Marian Bik, the second
Wladysław Bik, Joseph Bik and Mary Bik.
Wladysław and Maria still are living in
Cracow, where I am living to with my family.
 Thank you for your comming to
Krzemienica. It was the Great Day for
my Father. why?
Because lately he told a story to us
about yours family. Sometimes He was
talking with His friends about this terrible
time their youthfulness, they remember
yours family. When they were older, then
they more often remember this time.

We, means 'Marian's children, truely
belive, but we were a little bit sceptical,
We were sure that yours family has forgotten
it. We belive Father's story because
we had heard it from other different
people.

My Father was more happy with yours
visit, than He win a biggest money,
because it was really succes his
moral principles. He is a catholic and
is strong in His faith.

He and all our family would like to
~~say yours family~~ "Thank you for visit."
~~Add~~ now a few words about Josep
Bih, which bring yours ~~me~~ family member
to hide in our farm. I would like to
write, how Joseph Bih was killed.

Because He was a lieutentant Armii
Krajowej / Home Army — it was Polish
underground Army of the Resistance
movement during the Nazi occupation
in World War II called to life by the
National Peoples Councill.
After the World War II—d Joseph Bih

didn't see a possibility to live in Poland, because the comunistic police were looking for him, he decided emigrate to England. His command prepared to him escape to England with plane. But he went to the second village in purpose to say godd-by to Marian's mother and father-in-law. He spend there a few hours and sombody denounce him.

From MIELEC /the nearest town/ to arrive a secret political police from District Committee Communist Party with two car, 10 persons ~~with~~ authomatic ~~arms.~~

The farm where was Joseph, is lying on border of village. The police to enclose the farm around. They called him to give up. But he didn't. He knew that in this time in Poland was no justice, particunaly for Polish Home Army officers. He wouldn't be to put through an examination, for torture in jail and to take sentence in prisonment and to death.

He decide to defend. He hide behind concrete well. The police start

shoot towards Him. [IIA] He defended only
with small pistol. The ammunition ended,
but the police were afraid to take Him aliv
because they knew that he was very
muscular and brave. They shoot Him with
authomatic arms a few bullets in stomac

They put Him to the car and went to
Mielec. On their way they stopped
at his Fathers Wojciech gate, called
all his family and keeping the family
against authomatic arms, one policem
cut catch his hair, pull up to show
his parents his head and told to
them " If somebody move we kill him
this is your hero". His mother try to g
to him. One of soldier shoot in the air
Joseph said " Don't move Mumy, this
beast kill you, I have to die, stay
with Good"

One soldier take off his shoes throw
on yard and said to his parents, Yours
hero no more needs them", and they
left. Joseph parents to try find out
what happened with his son, but nobody
tell them. Everybody was frightened.

112

After few month his brother Marians took a message from cementry workers where is his tomb. Joseph's family couldn't do nothing with this tomb, event care about. Barely in 1956 /it was the first demonstration against communist rule in Poland in Poznan town/. The Bik's family made an ext exhumation to be sure that it was this tomb. And realy it was. But Joseph's parent died early, and they never know it.

In all this tragedy was nice to know where is Joseph's tomb, because plenty of people was killed and till now nobody knows where are their tombs.

In 1956 Marian's family had 5 children, his wife (my mother Jernina) was sick and we have no money to do some monuments. We did it in 1975. In 1960 in our village was built a monument for people whi which was killed by Nazi. In 1990 after falling down of communizm Association of Figthers for Liberty and Democracy decide to put the table of memory Joseph's Bik. And they did it. After so many years young people in our village knows much more about when I, when I was young.

Now all people [34] killed by Nazi, killed by Russian and killed by Polish Communis[t] are equel, and this is a strange decree of fate.

<u>Dear Debbie and Michael!</u>

Don't send to us any money, dress and toys. I know it is troublesome. We no are not rich, but we are not pure to.

But do some favour for my Father. Lets tell the Huna to write down som declaration that marian Bik born in Krzemienica District Mielec to save mem[b] yours family, and da this declaration ~~against public notary~~. In next letter I will write you why. My Father is now in hospital and we need this declaration for better sex medical service. Do it immediately as is possible. I ask you strongly.

Now I finish this letter, in nex[t] I am going to write a little bit more about our familly.

Your sincerely Bik's fami[ly]
your sincerely Sta[n]

My adres is:
STANISLAW BIK
ul. NADZIEJA 10
30-645 KRAKÓW   POLAND.   in Cracov 21. 05. 1994ĸ.

114

Chapter Eight

Memorial To Amir

When I spoke at the theater presentation of immigration, "Coming Through" – the Ellis Island project, this was the story that I shared with the audience – my quest to find the family that saved my life – to thank them. The joy of our wonderful reunion and the proof that there are wonderful human beings in this world – people of any color, creed, or religion. One just has to be lucky enough to find them. And I did.

This whole episode and the Heritage trip to find my Jewish roots brought me back to some special moments I had spent with Amir Meytal.

The Lebanese War was now over and Amir could technically leave the army and start his life as a civilian. He had this choice: He was twenty-eight years old and had his whole life ahead of him. But for Amir, the responsibility to his country weighed heavily on him.

There was a time when Amir was in the U.S. on holiday, he and our daughter Michelle spent some time together. One day they sat together on a beach just enjoying this special time together, reminiscing about their lives when suddenly Amir turned to her and said, "you know Michelle, sometimes, I wish I could be like you and your friends – free without a care in the world." To

Amir on vacation in the U.S.

which Michelle answered, "Amir, you've already done your duty. You could leave the army at any time." But he told her he couldn't. "If not for me and people like me, who will defend the country?" That was Amir Meytal.

There was a time when he sat with me in my living room and asked me to tell him about my childhood and about the Holocaust. He wanted to know how did I survive the war. His curiosity and interest took me by surprise. I told him that most young people his age were really not that interested in hearing such stories anymore. But he insisted. He wanted to know all about the history of his people and for whom he was fighting. This was Amir Meytal.

One of the stories I told Amir was about an episode that happened to me a few years back. In these years, there wasn't much awareness and teaching of the Holocaust as there is today. I, in particular had not delved into my past and I didn't think the past had any effect on me.

But one day, my daughter Debbie's first grade put on a play on Yom HaShoa and of course all the parents were invited to attend.

I got dressed, put on my makeup, did up my hair and set out to see my child in a school play, not giving it any further thought. When I arrived at school, it was still early and so I began to glance at the photos and drawings on the wall. There were pictures that were drawn by the children of the concentration camp Terrezenstadt. Without realizing it, I began to feel more and more uncomfortable.

Michelle and Amir in New York

Till now I really did not give much thought to where I came from, or who I really was. The way I saw myself – I was this young mother of a six-year old American born child coming to watch her daughter perform in a play. I certainly was not prepared for what happened to me next. I entered the darkened room and what I saw were the children, my daughter among them wearing all black outfits and pinned on their chest was a yellow star of David. The

sight of the yellow star brought back all the terrible memories and feelings that I didn't realize I even possessed. It was one thing for me to live through this terrible period but to see my child wearing a yellow star was more than I could bear. I became hysterical. I was totally uncontrollable. I had to run out of that room.

This was the first time since the war that I became

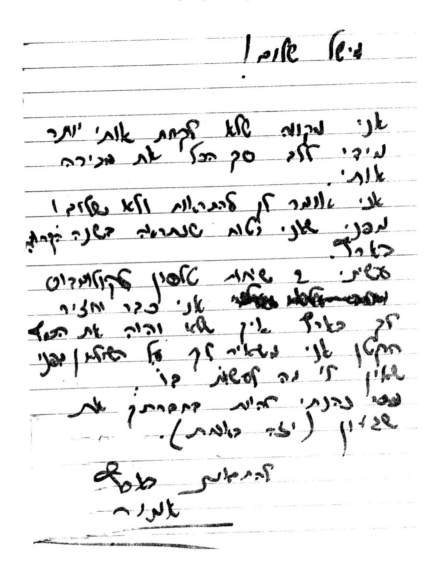

Amir's parting letter to Michelle

aware of my sub-conscious feelings. The feelings that were buried so deep that I could not face them. And now they were out and I could not contain myself.

I was asked many times to speak publicly about my past but I realize now that I still can't do it. The minute I start to speak, tears fill my eyes and I can't utter an-

Amir Meytal

other word. I did however give a deposition to Steven Spielberg several years later. This too was very painful albeit very necessary.

Perhaps I've finally realized the time has come to write this memoir – a memoir for my children and their spouses, for my grandchildren and especially for Amir Meytal.

Amir liked to joke about the fact that we had hosted Ariel Sharon in our home. He would quip "you think Sharon is somebody, one day you will know who is Amir Meytal." And the day came when we knew.

Amir went back to Israel at the end of his officer's training course and this beautiful vacation. He went back into the Army, was promoted to the rank of Lieutenant Colonel, and at the young age of twenty-nine, became the commander of a whole battalion of soldiers.

We were all so proud as were his parents, Rifka and David, as well as his brother Shai and sister Michal and her husband Ellie and the whole town of Hadera.

Unfortunately, all this joy and happiness came to a sudden and tragic end.

The telephone call that we never wanted to receive came from Amir's father David. Thursday night, December 1989. The telephone startled us out of a deep sleep. Irwin and I both grabbed the receiver but all we could hear at the other end was a trembling voice and the words "Amir dead." Irwin and I thought we were dreaming – a terrible nightmare we thought.

We couldn't believe what we were hearing. Our minds couldn't comprehend the words we were hearing. This was not happening. But, unfortunately it was happening and the sad reality of this horrible tragedy began to sink in. Irwin and I would have done anything in the world not to hear this terrible news. Saturday night found me on an El Al flight to Israel for Amir's funeral. It was the saddest trip I had ever made.

Amir had volunteered for a very dangerous mission deep into Lebanon. He didn't have to go but he felt that he knew the terrain better than anyone and he was the commander and the leader and leaders have to lead. And so we lost a beautiful soul. An Israeli Sabra, tough on the outside but sweet and soft and caring on the inside. Amir who was like a son to us and who would joke and tell everyone that he had one mother in Israel and one mother in America was no more. Amir, who for us represented the best of the best of Israel was gone – and with him a part of all of us was gone as well. Our life would never be the same again. Israel for us would never be the same again.

About a year later in 1990, I was invited to a private meeting on behalf of the Anti-Defamation League an organization that Irwin and I support. The guest speaker was Yitzhak Rabin, then running for the office of the Prime Minister to which he was elected a few months later. Before he gave his presentation he came up to me and said, "I think we've met before but I can't remember where." To which I replied, "Yes, we did meet. It was at the home of Rifka and David Meytal at the Shiva for Amir." He was stunned. To be in a home in Lawrence, N.Y. and to meet someone who had such a

Esther Weber and Yitzhak Rabin

special connection with an Israeli Hero, a Golani Soldier. I could see the pain in his eyes when he spoke of Amir and the terrible loss we've all endured. This was the love and honor and respect that Amir commanded and received from the simplest foot soldier to the highest ranking General such as Yitzhak Rabin.

Years later, on June 11, 1991, Aviva and David had their third child – a boy. They named him "Amir Shlomo." When the rabbi announced the baby's name, we were all taken by surprise and needless to say very emotional. But knowing Aviva and David and their love for Amir, we really shouldn't have been surprised at all. They also gave him an English name, Joshua.

A few years ago, when it was our grandson Avi's Bar Mitzvah, and time to put on his tefillin at the Kotel HaMaaravi, Aviva and David, Irwin and I and Daniella and Josh all accompanied Avi to Israel to celebrate this special occasion.

This became the tradition in the Weber Family. We later went to visit Amir's grave as was our custom.

Josh (Amir Shlomo) with Aunt Selly

While standing at the cemetery saying Kaddish, a strange man came over to us and asked us who we were and what was our relationship to Amir Meytal. We proceeded to explain and also to introduce Josh to him and to share with him our story. We told him that Amir was our son David's childhood friend and that when his son was born, he named him "Amir" in memory of his dear friend.

With that, the man, who we later found out also lost

123

David, Aviva, Daniella, Josh, and I at Amir's gravesite

his own son in the war, picked Josh up in his arms and proceeded to explain to Josh exactly who he was named for – that Amir was one of the great heroes of Israel and that had he lived, he might even have become Prime Minister one day.

"And so Josh, know that you are named for one of the great defenders of Israel – a martyr who gave his life so that others may live. A hero who will be remembered for his bravery and dedication to his country and to his people and last but not least, your father's dear friend, Lieutenant Colonel Amir Meytal."

An article by Deborah Weber

"Peace, peace – yet there is no peace . . ." This quote, which I have taken from Jeremiah 6:14, reflects the events transpiring in the Middle East today. The Jewish state of Israel, the only democracy in the Middle East, is surrounded by the Mediterranean Sea on one side and the Arab countries of Lebanon, Syria, Jordan and Egypt on the other. These Arab countries are auspices for terrorists and provide asylum for terrorists such as Abu Nidal and Ahmed Gabril. These barbaric men are among thousands who organize and operate violent and deathly activities, one of which was responsible for taking the beautiful, bright, life of Amir Meytal, someone who was like a brother to me.

The time that I spent living in Israel with family and friends caused me to be more aware of the events prevailing around me with which I was in close proximity. Israelis, being the prey to incessant occurrences of Arab terrorism, frequently attack those who committed the heinous crimes as a means of retaliation. Amir was a proud, dedicated, career, elite army Lieutenant who was killed in combat defending Israel in Lebanon, a year ago this month. I had the honor of knowing Amir all my life. Seeing him when he would come home from his base was always a treat for the town of Hadera.

Not only because he was such a high ranking military persona, but because in Hadera he was still the genial, light-hearted, Amir who returned for some good food, a warm home and a soft bed. It was Amir whom everyone missed and worried about for the duration of days he was away on missions.

Amir was loved by everyone and was understandably considered an asset to the state of Israel.

As I laid a flower on Amir's grave I recalled the moments we shared together growing up. I remembered playing on the beach. I remembered his dignified, patriotic image. I remembered attending his graduation from military academy when I was a little girl. I remembered his visit to America and his stay in my home. Today, I think of a martyr who died too soon before his time. Amir should have grown old; he should have become an old general who would live to tell military stories to his grandchildren. But Amir left behind no wife or children, only a bereaving family. Amir's death was a loss to all who knew him and especially to the State of Israel.

In the Hadera cemetery, there is an area for military heroes who fell in the line of duty. As I stood in front of Amir's resting place, I looked to the right and noticed that the rest of the area was empty; there were no more graves. I silently asked G-d to never fill up that or any other military cemetery; I asked for a termination of war.

Amir would not have tolerated anyone grieving for him because he felt serving the country was a duty. He was even known on occasion to say that inevitably, he would be killed and someone else would take his place. This was a concept that Amir lived with every day. Yet I have difficulty dealing with it.

When does all the bloodshed end? What angers me the most is that these inhumane Arab terrorists took Amir's and countless other's lives and the circle continues and there is still no peace.

Chapter Nine

Triumph Over Adversity

S o to you Adolph Hitler I say, you have tried very hard to destroy the Jewish people but you have failed miserably. We are still here and we'll continue to grow and multiply and follow a beautiful Torah way of life.

With three wonderful children, David, Michelle, and Debbie and their wonderful spouses and ten grandchildren, these are some of our recent happy occasions:

Debbie, David, and Michelle